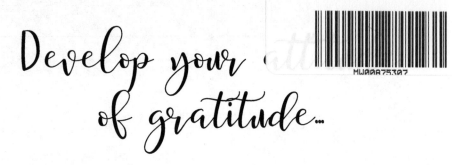

Develop your attitude of gratitude...

If you enjoy our journal and want to show your gratitude, please support us by writing a review!

There is an increasing body of research findings, showing that developing an attitude of gratitude can have all kinds of benefits.

Some of the benefits this research suggests includes: improvements in physical and psychological health, better relationships, self-esteem, empathy, and resilience.

Start today, and begin to notice little positives in every day to be grateful for. You might start to appreciate little moments of gratitude like a sunny day, being kind to someone or even the smell of fresh coffee.

This journal helps to you record and track moments to be grateful for each day. There is also space for reflection and review after seven days, and after every four weeks.

So, get going and get grateful!

If you enjoy our journal and want to show your gratitude, please support us by writing a review.

Date:_____

Today I am grateful for:

_____

_____

_____

Date:_____

Today I am grateful for:

_____

_____

_____

Date:_____

Today I am grateful for:

_____

_____

_____

Date:_____

Today I am grateful for:

_____

_____

_____

Date:_____

Today I am grateful for:

_____

_____

_____

Date:_____

Today I am grateful for:

_____

_____

_____

Date:_____

Today I am grateful for:

_____

_____

_____

Seven Day Reflection

What have I been most grateful for this week? Tick and comment:

- Myself
- Health/Wellbeing
- Friends/Family
- Leisure time
- Achievements
- Food/drink
- Other

Reflection/Comments:

_____

_____

_____

> *There is nothing I would not do for those who are really my friends*
>
> Jane Austen

Date:_____

Today I am grateful for:

_____

_____

_____

Date:_____

Today I am grateful for:

_____

_____

_____

Date:_____

Today I am grateful for:

_____

_____

_____

Date:_____

Today I am grateful for:

_____

_____

_____

Date:_____

Today I am grateful for:

_____

_____

_____

Date:_____

Today I am grateful for:

_____

_____

_____

Date:_____

Today I am grateful for:

_____

_____

_____

Seven Day Reflection

What have I been most grateful for this week? Tick and comment:

- Myself
- Health/Wellbeing
- Friends/Family
- Leisure time
- Achievements
- Food/drink
- Other

Reflection/Comments:

_____

_____

_____

> *Don't spoil what you have by desiring what you don't have*
>
> Epicurus

Date:_____

Today I am grateful for:

_____

_____

_____

Date:_____

Today I am grateful for:

_____

_____

_____

Date:_____

Today I am grateful for:

_____

_____

_____

Date:_____

Today I am grateful for:

_____

_____

_____

Date:_____

Today I am grateful for:

_____

_____

_____

Date:_____

Today I am grateful for:

_____

_____

_____

Date:_____

Today I am grateful for:

_____

_____

_____

Seven Day Reflection

What have I been most grateful for this week? Tick and comment:

- [ ] Myself
- [ ] Health/Wellbeing
- [ ] Friends/Family
- [ ] Leisure time
- [ ] Achievements
- [ ] Food/drink
- [ ] Other

Reflection/Comments:

_____

_____

_____

Date:_____

Today I am grateful for:

_____

_____

_____

Date:_____

Today I am grateful for:

_____

_____

_____

Date:_____

Today I am grateful for:

_____

_____

_____

Date:_____

Today I am grateful for:

_____

_____

_____

Date:_____

Today I am grateful for:

_____

_____

_____

Date:_____

Today I am grateful for:

_____

_____

_____

Date:_____

Today I am grateful for:

_____

_____

_____

Review and Goal Setting

What have I learned so far?

_____

_____

_____

What progress have I made so far?

_____

_____

_____

What goals or intentions would I like to set next?

_____

_____

_____

> *True happiness is to enjoy the present*
>
> Seneca

Date:_____

Today I am grateful for:

_____

_____

_____

Date:_____

Today I am grateful for:

_____

_____

_____

Date:_____

Today I am grateful for:

_____

_____

_____

Date:_____

Today I am grateful for:

_____

_____

_____

Date:_____

Today I am grateful for:

_____

_____

_____

Date:_____

Today I am grateful for:

_____

_____

_____

Date:_____

Today I am grateful for:

_____

_____

_____

Seven Day Reflection

What have I been most grateful for this week? Tick and comment:

- Myself
- Health/Wellbeing
- Friends/Family
- Leisure time
- Achievements
- Food/drink
- Other

Reflection/Comments:

_____

_____

_____

Appreciation is a wonderful thing

Voltaire

Date:_____

Today I am grateful for:

_____

_____

_____

Date:_____

Today I am grateful for:

_____

_____

_____

Date:_____

Today I am grateful for:

_____

_____

_____

Date:_____

Today I am grateful for:

_____

_____

_____

Date:_____

Today I am grateful for:

_____

_____

_____

Date:_____

Today I am grateful for:

_____

_____

_____

Date:_____

Today I am grateful for:

_____

_____

_____

Seven Day Reflection

What have I been most grateful for this week? Tick and comment:

- [ ] Myself
- [ ] Health/Wellbeing
- [ ] Friends/Family
- [ ] Leisure time
- [ ] Achievements
- [ ] Food/drink
- [ ] Other

Reflection/Comments:

_____

_____

_____

> *Good actions give us strength and inspire good actions in others*
>
> Plato

Date:_____

Today I am grateful for:

_____

_____

_____

Date:_____

Today I am grateful for:

_____

_____

_____

Date:_____

Today I am grateful for:

_____

_____

_____

Date:_____

Today I am grateful for:

_____

_____

_____

Date:_____

Today I am grateful for:

_____

_____

_____

Date:_____

Today I am grateful for:

_____

_____

_____

Date:_____

Today I am grateful for:

_____

_____

_____

Seven Day Reflection

What have I been most grateful for this week? Tick and comment:

- Myself
- Health/Wellbeing
- Friends/Family
- Leisure time
- Achievements
- Food/drink
- Other

Reflection/Comments:

_____

_____

_____

Take hold of a good minute

Spanish Proverb

Date:_____

Today I am grateful for:

_____

_____

_____

Date:_____

Today I am grateful for:

_____

_____

_____

Date:_____

Today I am grateful for:

_____

_____

_____

Date:_____

Today I am grateful for:

_____

_____

_____

Date:_____

Today I am grateful for:

_____

_____

_____

Date:_____

Today I am grateful for:

_____

_____

_____

Date:_____

Today I am grateful for:

_____

_____

_____

Review and Goal Setting

What have I learned recently?

_____

_____

_____

What progress have I made so far?

_____

_____

_____

What goals or intentions would I like to set next?

_____

_____

_____

> # What sunshine is to flowers, smiles are to humanity
>
> Joseph Addison

Date:_____

Today I am grateful for:

_____

_____

_____

Date:_____

Today I am grateful for:

_____

_____

_____

Date:_____

Today I am grateful for:

_____

_____

_____

Date:_____

Today I am grateful for:

_____

_____

_____

Date:_____

Today I am grateful for:

_____

_____

_____

Date:_____

Today I am grateful for:

_____

_____

_____

Date:_____

Today I am grateful for:

_____

_____

_____

Seven Day Reflection

What have I been most grateful for this week? Tick and comment:

- ☐ Myself
- ☐ Health/Wellbeing
- ☐ Friends/Family
- ☐ Leisure time
- ☐ Achievements
- ☐ Food/drink
- ☐ Other

Reflection/Comments:

_____

_____

_____

Enough is as good as a feast

Sir Thomas Malory

Date:_____

Today I am grateful for:

_____

_____

_____

Date:_____

Today I am grateful for:

_____

_____

_____

Date:_____

Today I am grateful for:

_____

_____

_____

Date:_____

Today I am grateful for:

_____

_____

_____

Date:_____

Today I am grateful for:

_____

_____

_____

Date:_____

Today I am grateful for:

_____

_____

_____

Date:_____

Today I am grateful for:

_____

_____

_____

Seven Day Reflection

What have I been most grateful for this week? Tick and comment:

- Myself
- Health/Wellbeing
- Friends/Family
- Leisure time
- Achievements
- Food/drink
- Other

Reflection/Comments:

_____

_____

_____

> # A grateful mind is a great mind
>
> Plato

Date:_____

Today I am grateful for:

_____

_____

_____

Date:_____

Today I am grateful for:

_____

_____

_____

Date:_____

Today I am grateful for:

_____

_____

_____

Date:_____

Today I am grateful for:

_____

_____

_____

Date:_____

Today I am grateful for:

_____

_____

_____

Date:_____

Today I am grateful for:

_____

_____

_____

Date:_____

Today I am grateful for:

_____

_____

_____

Seven Day Reflection

What have I been most grateful for this week? Tick and comment:

- [ ] Myself
- [ ] Health/Wellbeing
- [ ] Friends/Family
- [ ] Leisure time
- [ ] Achievements
- [ ] Food/drink
- [ ] Other

Reflection/Comments:

_____

_____

_____

> *Forget injuries, never forget kindness*
>
> Confucius

Date:_____

Today I am grateful for:

_____

_____

_____

Date:_____

Today I am grateful for:

_____

_____

_____

Date:_____

Today I am grateful for:

_____

_____

_____

Date:_____

Today I am grateful for:

_____

_____

_____

Date:_____

Today I am grateful for:

_____

_____

_____

Date:_____

Today I am grateful for:

_____

_____

_____

Date:_____

Today I am grateful for:

_____

_____

_____

Review and Goal Setting

What have I learned recently?

_____

_____

_____

What progress have I made so far?

_____

_____

_____

What goals or intentions would I like to set next?

_____

_____

_____

Thanks costs nothing

Creole Proverb

Date:_____

Today I am grateful for:

_____

_____

_____

Date:_____

Today I am grateful for:

_____

_____

_____

Date:_____

Today I am grateful for:

_____

_____

_____

Date:_____

Today I am grateful for:

_____

_____

_____

Date:_____

Today I am grateful for:

_____

_____

_____

Date:_____

Today I am grateful for:

_____

_____

_____

Date:_____

Today I am grateful for:

_____

_____

_____

Seven Day Reflection

What have I been most grateful for this week? Tick and comment:

- ☐ Myself
- ☐ Health/Wellbeing
- ☐ Friends/Family
- ☐ Leisure time
- ☐ Achievements
- ☐ Food/drink
- ☐ Other

Reflection/Comments:

_____

_____

_____

Fragrance clings to the hand that gives flowers

Chinese Proverb

Date:_____

Today I am grateful for:

_____

_____

_____

Date:_____

Today I am grateful for:

_____

_____

_____

Date:_____

Today I am grateful for:

_____

_____

_____

Date:_____

Today I am grateful for:

_____

_____

_____

Date:_____

Today I am grateful for:

_____

_____

_____

Date:_____

Today I am grateful for:

_____

_____

_____

Date:_____

Today I am grateful for:

_____

_____

_____

Seven Day Reflection

What have I been most grateful for this week? Tick and comment:

- Myself
- Health/Wellbeing
- Friends/Family
- Leisure time
- Achievements
- Food/drink
- Other

Reflection/Comments:

_____

_____

_____

We are shaped by our thoughts

Buddha

Date:_____

Today I am grateful for:

_____

_____

_____

Date:_____

Today I am grateful for:

_____

_____

_____

Date:_____

Today I am grateful for:

_____

_____

_____

Date:_____

Today I am grateful for:

_____

_____

_____

Date:_____

Today I am grateful for:

_____

_____

_____

Date:_____

Today I am grateful for:

_____

_____

_____

Date:_____

Today I am grateful for:

_____

_____

_____

Seven Day Reflection

What have I been most grateful for this week? Tick and comment:

- Myself
- Health/Wellbeing
- Friends/Family
- Leisure time
- Achievements
- Food/drink
- Other

Reflection/Comments:

_____

_____

_____

> *Love all, trust a few,*
> *do wrong to none.*
>
> William Shakespeare

Date:_____

Today I am grateful for:

_____

_____

_____

Date:_____

Today I am grateful for:

_____

_____

_____

Date:_____

Today I am grateful for:

_____

_____

_____

Date:_____

Today I am grateful for:

_____

_____

_____

Date:_____

Today I am grateful for:

_____

_____

_____

Date:_____

Today I am grateful for:

_____

_____

_____

Date:_____

Today I am grateful for:

_____

_____

_____

Review and Goal Setting

What have I learned recently?

_____

_____

_____

What progress have I made so far?

_____

_____

_____

What goals or intentions would I like to set next?

_____

_____

_____

Gratitude is the heart's memory

French Proverb

Date:_____

Today I am grateful for:

_____

_____

_____

Date:_____

Today I am grateful for:

_____

_____

_____

Date:_____

Today I am grateful for:

_____

_____

_____

Date:_____

Today I am grateful for:

_____

_____

_____

Date:_____

Today I am grateful for:

_____

_____

_____

Date:_____

Today I am grateful for:

_____

_____

_____

Date:_____

Today I am grateful for:

_____

_____

_____

Seven Day Reflection

What have I been most grateful for this week? Tick and comment:

- [ ] Myself
- [ ] Health/Wellbeing
- [ ] Friends/Family
- [ ] Leisure time
- [ ] Achievements
- [ ] Food/drink
- [ ] Other

Reflection/Comments:

_____

_____

_____

We can complain because rose bushes have thorns or rejoice because thorns have roses

Alphonse Karr

Date: _____

Today I am grateful for:

_____

_____

_____

Date: _____

Today I am grateful for:

_____

_____

_____

Date: _____

Today I am grateful for:

_____

_____

_____

Date:_____

Today I am grateful for:

_____

_____

_____

Date:_____

Today I am grateful for:

_____

_____

_____

Date:_____

Today I am grateful for:

_____

_____

_____

Date:_____

Today I am grateful for:

_____

_____

_____

Seven Day Reflection

What have I been most grateful for this week? Tick and comment:

- Myself
- Health/Wellbeing
- Friends/Family
- Leisure time
- Achievements
- Food/drink
- Other

Reflection/Comments:

_____

_____

_____

Date:_____

Today I am grateful for:

_____

_____

_____

Date:_____

Today I am grateful for:

_____

_____

_____

Date:_____

Today I am grateful for:

_____

_____

_____

Date:_____

Today I am grateful for:

_____

_____

_____

Date:_____

Today I am grateful for:

_____

_____

_____

Date:_____

Today I am grateful for:

_____

_____

_____

Date:_____

Today I am grateful for:

_____

_____

_____

Seven Day Reflection

What have I been most grateful for this week? Tick and comment:

- [ ] Myself
- [ ] Health/Wellbeing
- [ ] Friends/Family
- [ ] Leisure time
- [ ] Achievements
- [ ] Food/drink
- [ ] Other

Reflection/Comments:

_____

_____

_____

Date:_____

Today I am grateful for:

_____

_____

_____

Date:_____

Today I am grateful for:

_____

_____

_____

Date:_____

Today I am grateful for:

_____

_____

_____

Date:_____

Today I am grateful for:

_____

_____

_____

Date:_____

Today I am grateful for:

_____

_____

_____

Date:_____

Today I am grateful for:

_____

_____

_____

Date:_____

Today I am grateful for:

_____

_____

_____

Review and Goal Setting

What have I learned recently?

_____

_____

_____

What progress have I made so far?

_____

_____

_____

What goals or intentions would I like to set next?

_____

_____

_____

> *You should include all things in your gratitude*
> Ralph Waldo Emerson

Date:_____

Today I am grateful for:

_____

_____

_____

Date:_____

Today I am grateful for:

_____

_____

_____

Date:_____

Today I am grateful for:

_____

_____

_____

Date:_____

Today I am grateful for:

_____

_____

_____

Date:_____

Today I am grateful for:

_____

_____

_____

Date:_____

Today I am grateful for:

_____

_____

_____

Date:_____

Today I am grateful for:

_____

_____

_____

Seven Day Reflection

What have I been most grateful for this week? Tick and comment:

- [ ] Myself
- [ ] Health/Wellbeing
- [ ] Friends/Family
- [ ] Leisure time
- [ ] Achievements
- [ ] Food/drink
- [ ] Other

Reflection/Comments:

_____

_____

_____

> *If the only prayer you said was thank you, that would be enough*

Date:_____

Today I am grateful for:

_____

_____

_____

Date:_____

Today I am grateful for:

_____

_____

_____

Date:_____

Today I am grateful for:

_____

_____

_____

Date:_____

Today I am grateful for:

_____

_____

_____

Date:_____

Today I am grateful for:

_____

_____

_____

Date:_____

Today I am grateful for:

_____

_____

_____

Date:_____

Today I am grateful for:

_____

_____

_____

Seven Day Reflection

What have I been most grateful for this week? Tick and comment:

- [ ] Myself
- [ ] Health/Wellbeing
- [ ] Friends/Family
- [ ] Leisure time
- [ ] Achievements
- [ ] Food/drink
- [ ] Other

Reflection/Comments:

_____

_____

_____

> *Gratitude is not only the greatest of virtues, but the parent of all others*
>
> Marcus Tullius Cicero

Date:_____

Today I am grateful for:

_____

_____

_____

Date:_____

Today I am grateful for:

_____

_____

_____

Date:_____

Today I am grateful for:

_____

_____

_____

Date:_____

Today I am grateful for:

_____

_____

_____

Date:_____

Today I am grateful for:

_____

_____

_____

Date:_____

Today I am grateful for:

_____

_____

_____

Date:_____

Today I am grateful for:

_____

_____

_____

Seven Day Reflection

What have I been most grateful for this week? Tick and comment:

- Myself
- Health/Wellbeing
- Friends/Family
- Leisure time
- Achievements
- Food/drink
- Other

Reflection/Comments:

_____

_____

_____

> *The thankful heart will find, in every hour, some heavenly blessings*
>
> Henry Ward Beecher

Date:_____

Today I am grateful for:

_____

_____

_____

Date:_____

Today I am grateful for:

_____

_____

_____

Date:_____

Today I am grateful for:

_____

_____

_____

Date:_____

Today I am grateful for:

_____

_____

_____

Date:_____

Today I am grateful for:

_____

_____

_____

Date:_____

Today I am grateful for:

_____

_____

_____

Date:_____

Today I am grateful for:

_____

_____

_____

Review and Goal Setting

What have I learned recently?

_____

_____

_____

What progress have I made so far?

_____

_____

_____

What goals or intentions would I like to set next?

_____

_____

_____

> *It isn't what we say or think that defines us, but what we do*
>
> Jane Austen

Date: _____

Today I am grateful for:

_____

_____

_____

Date: _____

Today I am grateful for:

_____

_____

_____

Date: _____

Today I am grateful for:

_____

_____

_____

Date:_____

Today I am grateful for:

_____

_____

_____

Date:_____

Today I am grateful for:

_____

_____

_____

Date:_____

Today I am grateful for:

_____

_____

_____

Date:_____

Today I am grateful for:

_____

_____

_____

Seven Day Reflection

What have I been most grateful for this week? Tick and comment:

- [ ] Myself
- [ ] Health/Wellbeing
- [ ] Friends/Family
- [ ] Leisure time
- [ ] Achievements
- [ ] Food/drink
- [ ] Other

Reflection/Comments:

_____

_____

_____

> *Only when you have eaten a lemon do you appreciate what sugar is*
>
> Ukranian Proverb

Date:_____

Today I am grateful for:

_____

_____

_____

Date:_____

Today I am grateful for:

_____

_____

_____

Date:_____

Today I am grateful for:

_____

_____

_____

Date:_____

Today I am grateful for:

_____

_____

_____

Date:_____

Today I am grateful for:

_____

_____

_____

Date:_____

Today I am grateful for:

_____

_____

_____

Date:_____

Today I am grateful for:

_____

_____

_____

Seven Day Reflection

What have I been most grateful for this week? Tick and comment:

- [ ] Myself
- [ ] Health/Wellbeing
- [ ] Friends/Family
- [ ] Leisure time
- [ ] Achievements
- [ ] Food/drink
- [ ] Other

Reflection/Comments:

_____

_____

_____

> *It is not the man who has too little, but the man who craves more, that is poor*
>
> Marcus Annaeus Seneca

Date:_____

Today I am grateful for:

_____

_____

_____

Date:_____

Today I am grateful for:

_____

_____

_____

Date:_____

Today I am grateful for:

_____

_____

_____

Date:_____

Today I am grateful for:

_____

_____

_____

Date:_____

Today I am grateful for:

_____

_____

_____

Date:_____

Today I am grateful for:

_____

_____

_____

Date:_____

Today I am grateful for:

_____

_____

_____

Seven Day Reflection

What have I been most grateful for this week? Tick and comment:

- Myself
- Health/Wellbeing
- Friends/Family
- Leisure time
- Achievements
- Food/drink
- Other

Reflection/Comments:

_____

_____

_____

> Do not dwell in the past, do not dream
> of the future, concentrate the mind
> on the present moment
>
> Budda

Date:_____

Today I am grateful for:

_____

_____

_____

Date:_____

Today I am grateful for:

_____

_____

_____

Date:_____

Today I am grateful for:

_____

_____

_____

Date:_____

Today I am grateful for:

_____

_____

_____

Date:_____

Today I am grateful for:

_____

_____

_____

Date:_____

Today I am grateful for:

_____

_____

_____

Date:_____

Today I am grateful for:

_____

_____

_____

Review and Goal Setting

What have I learned recently?

_____

_____

_____

What progress have I made so far?

_____

_____

_____

What goals or intentions would I like to set next?

_____

_____

_____

Happiness depends upon ourselves

Aristotle

Date:_____

Today I am grateful for:

_____

_____

_____

Date:_____

Today I am grateful for:

_____

_____

_____

Date:_____

Today I am grateful for:

_____

_____

_____

Date:_____

Today I am grateful for:

_____

_____

_____

Date:_____

Today I am grateful for:

_____

_____

_____

Date:_____

Today I am grateful for:

_____

_____

_____

Date:_____

Today I am grateful for:

_____

_____

_____

Seven Day Reflection

What have I been most grateful for this week? Tick and comment:

- [ ] Myself
- [ ] Health/Wellbeing
- [ ] Friends/Family
- [ ] Leisure time
- [ ] Achievements
- [ ] Food/drink
- [ ] Other

Reflection/Comments:

_____

_____

_____

The essence of all beautiful art,

all great art, is gratitude.

Date:_____

Today I am grateful for:

_____

_____

_____

Date:_____

Today I am grateful for:

_____

_____

_____

Date:_____

Today I am grateful for:

_____

_____

_____

Date:_____

Today I am grateful for:

_____

_____

_____

Date:_____

Today I am grateful for:

_____

_____

_____

Date:_____

Today I am grateful for:

_____

_____

_____

Date:_____

Today I am grateful for:

_____

_____

_____

Seven Day Reflection

What have I been most grateful for this week? Tick and comment:

- [ ] Myself
- [ ] Health/Wellbeing
- [ ] Friends/Family
- [ ] Leisure time
- [ ] Achievements
- [ ] Food/drink
- [ ] Other

Reflection/Comments:

_____

_____

_____

Gratitude is the best attitude

Joseph Addison

Date: _____

Today I am grateful for:

_____

_____

_____

Date: _____

Today I am grateful for:

_____

_____

_____

Date: _____

Today I am grateful for:

_____

_____

_____

Date:_____

Today I am grateful for:

_____

_____

_____

Date:_____

Today I am grateful for:

_____

_____

_____

Date:_____

Today I am grateful for:

_____

_____

_____

Date:_____

Today I am grateful for:

_____

_____

_____

Seven Day Reflection

What have I been most grateful for this week? Tick and comment:

- Myself
- Health/Wellbeing
- Friends/Family
- Leisure time
- Achievements
- Food/drink
- Other

Reflection/Comments:

_____

_____

_____

Congratulations!

You have completed the Gratitude Journal!

Look back to Day 1. How have things changed since then?

_____

_____

_____

What are you looking forward to?

_____

_____

_____

Made in United States
Orlando, FL
08 June 2023